Preface: A New Era

Those who cannot learn from history are doomed to repeat it.
-George Santayana

0.1   What this Book Offers

On March 2016, the SAT Math section will undergo some major changes. It will

- Introduce Non-Calculator Math Sections.

- Change Multiple Choice Questions to have only 4 Choices.

- Remove the Guessing Penalty.

But the biggest change to the SAT Math section is the *additional content*. These new topics include a lot more algebra, some more geometry, and a sprinkle of trigonometry. In particular, you may see questions testing you on the nature of polynomial roots, lengths of chords, and the relationship between cosine and sine. But even though people may think that the new SAT mathematics is a completely different exam, the truth is,

You Will Still Be Tested on the Fundamentals

Pythagorean Theorem is *still* Pythagorean Theorem. You will *still* need to know the basics of 30-60-90 triangles, algebraic manipulations, and number properties. These are the fundamentals of high school mathematics and they will *always* be tested. And even though there will be *additional* content, **they will not discard the fundamentals that were tested on previous exams**.

Now one may argue that the SAT has been redesigned to be *less tricky* than the old SAT. But the truth is,

The College Board never believed its problems were too difficult or meant to trick people.

Just check the back cover of the classic College Board Blue Book. The company states, in gigantic bold letters, that "[it is a myth] that SAT questions are designed to trick students." And I agree. The *few* problems that has earned the SAT Math this reputation are simply math concepts tested in a *creative* way. And just like the original SAT, there will always be a few problems that will require deeper thinking, distinguishing the students who score a 700 with those who score an 800.

What I have done is that I have amassed a collection of all these "tricky" problems from the last ten years of SAT exams. These are the questions that the *majority* of my students have missed when they have taken these tests. I then reincarnated these questions in the format of the new SAT.

0.2   How Exactly are these Questions Reincarnated?

In order to train the world's top mathematicians, the *Art of Problem Solving Series* collects and publishes specific problems from the American Math Competition. Unfortunately, I do not have the same liberty (unless I wish to incur the wrath of the College Board company). So instead, I took each SAT problem and rewrote it so that it fits the format of the new SAT and has the same *essence* as its previous incarnation.

For example, consider the final question[1] on the October 2011 exam:

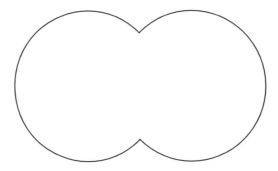

The figure above is made up of two identical 270° arcs. Each arc is part of a circle of radius 8.
What is the area of the figure?

A. 96π

B. $128\pi + 6$

C. $48\pi + 64$

D. $96\pi + 32$

E. $96\pi + 64$

The key to this frequently missed problem is to draw axillary lines and see that the figure is composed of two sectors and a square:

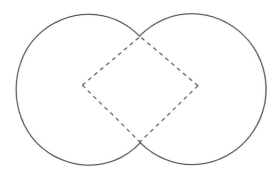

To reincarnate this problem, I kept the concept (arc lengths and sectors) as well as the "trick" (drawing auxiliary lines), and removed one of the answer choices to fit the new SAT format:

---

[1]This is the only problem from the College Board that I dare to write verbatim in this book.

Suppose a circle has a 60° arc removed. Then, the endpoints of the remaining arc are connected with a line segment to create the following shape:

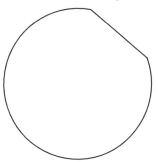

If the original circle had a radius of 6, then what is the perimeter of this shape?

A. 10π

B. $10\pi + 6$

C. 12π

D. $12\pi + 6$

Again, the trick is to draw auxiliary lines and interpret the figure as part of a circle and an equilateral triangle:

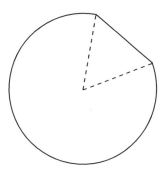

0.3 Who Should Read This Book?

DO NOT read this book if

- **You are a B+ math student who wants to break a 700.**
  I highly encourage you to look through Mr. Khan's website and watch his videos to learn the math fundamentals. This book is only for those who *mastered* the fundamentals and want to see the creative ways in which these concepts have appeared in the past.

- **You are looking for SAT practice tests.**
  This book only contains the *hardest* questions from a multitude of past SAT exams. The majority of real SAT questions are far easier. For practice tests of the new March 2016 exam, I recommend Princeton Review or Kaplan.

- **You are looking for a book that has the hardest problems based on the new content.** Unfortunately there are only 4 available practice tests from the College Board with only a few difficult problems from each.[2] After the first year in which these exams are released; however, I will update this text to have 300 problems incorporating all content.

DO READ this book if

- **You are an A+ student who wants to go from 700 to a perfect score.**

- **You understand the mathematics, but miss only the "tricky" questions on each test.**

- **You do not want to waste your time on "fodder" problems.**

For the SAT Math (and mathematics in general), there is no better way to improve than practicing problems. Especially if those problems are non-trivial and frequently missed by the top students.

0.4   Special Thanks

I would like to thank all of my SAT students: from their exams, I was able to amass this spectacular collection of frequently missed questions. I would also like to give special thanks to the students who edited and beta tested these problems, specifically, Fiona Sequeria, who has had an inordinate amount of patience. I hope that from my students' hard work and mistakes, these problems can benefit all students trying to get the perfect score.

---

[2]In particular, there is a really nifty non-calculator question which requires invoking the rational roots theorem.

Chapter 1

Numbers

1.1 Integers

1. **(October 2005)** Define
$$f(x) = \frac{x^2 + 1}{x - 2}.$$
If $f(n)$ is an integer for some integer n, which can be the value of $f(n)$?

   I. 10

  II. -2

 III. 1

   A. *I* only

   B. *II* only

   C. *I, II* only

   D. *I, II* and *III*.

2. **(January 2006)** On a list of 8 integers, suppose that the smallest number on the list is 1, the median is 3.5, and the mode is 2. If the average of the list is 7, what is the greatest possible number that can be on this list?

   A. 30

   B. 31

   C. 32

   D. 33

3. (**May 2006**) A *perfect* number is an integer that is a sum of its positive divisors, excluding the number itself. Which of the numbers below is *perfect*?

    A. 10

    B. 15

    C. 20

    D. 28

4. (**October 2006**) If m leaves a remainder of 5 when divided by 6 and n leaves a remainder of 2 when divided by 9, what is the remainder of mn when divided by 3?

5. (**January 2007**) A number x is called a *perfect square* if

$$x = k^2$$

for some integer k. How many positive integers less than 19 can be written as a sum of two positive perfect squares?

    A. 6

    B. 7

    C. 8

    D. 9

6. (**October 2007**) If, for positive integers w, x, y and z, we have

$$w + \frac{x}{2} + \frac{y}{4} + \frac{z}{8} = 2$$

Then what is the value of $w + x + y + z$?

7. (**October 2008**) If n is an integer, what is the difference between the smallest and greatest possible n that satisfies

$$n^2 < 24 - 14n$$

    A. 8

    B. 9

    C. 10

    D. 14

8. (**October 2009**) Let E be the sum of the first 100 positive even numbers and S be the sum of the first 100 positive multiples of 6. What is $\dfrac{S}{E}$?

9. (**January 2010**) If a is the product of three distinct integers greater than 10 and b is the product of three distinct integers less than 12, then what is the smallest possible value of $\dfrac{a}{b}$?

    A. $\frac{26}{15}$

    B. $\frac{27}{16}$

    C. $\frac{28}{17}$

    D. $\frac{29}{19}$

10. (**May 2010**) Suppose a, b and c are distinct positive integers such that

$$a^3 = b$$
$$9b = c^2$$

    What is the smallest possible value for c?

    A. 10

    B. 15

    C. 24

    D. 30

11. (**October 2012**) Suppose we have a list of 15 consecutive odd integers. If the average of this list is 21, what is the largest number on this list?

    A. 21

    B. 29

    C. 33

    D. 35

12. (**Bluebook**) On a list of consecutive even integers, suppose that -42 is the smallest number on this list. If the sum of all the numbers on this list is 90, then how many numbers are on this list?

    A. 42

    B. 43

    C. 44

    D. 45

1.2   Evens and Odds

13. **(January 2008)** Suppose

$$x^2 - y^2$$

is odd for some integers x and y. Which must be true?

    I. $x - y$ is odd.

   II. $x + y$ is even.

  III. xy is odd.

   A. I only

   B. II only

   C. I and III only

   D. I, II, and III

14. **(October 2009)** Let S be the sum of all even numbers from 2 to 100 (inclusive) and D be the sum of all odd numbers from 1 to 99 (inclusive):

$$
\begin{aligned}
S &= 2 + 4 + 6 + \ldots + 100 \\
D &= 1 + 3 + 5 + \ldots + 99
\end{aligned}
$$

What is $S - D$?

15. **(January 2010)** For integers x and y, we say (x, y) is an integer pair solution to an equation if it makes that equation true. How many integer pair solutions does

$$4x + 6y = 71$$

have?

   A. 0

   B. 1

   C. 2

   D. More than 2

16. (**October 2011**) If n is an odd integer, which must also be odd?

> I $n + 2$
>
> II $\dfrac{n - 1}{2}$
>
> III n^n

   A. I only

   B. II only

   C. I and III

   D. I, II, and III

17. (**Bluebook**) Which of the following is always 1 more than double an even number?

   A. $n + 1$

   B. $2n + 1$

   C. $4n + 1$

   D. $4n + 3$

1.3 Primes

18. (**May 2005**) Suppose s satisfies the property that

$$s = p^2$$

for some prime number p greater than 3. How many positive factors does $2s^2$ have?

   A. 5

   B. 10

   C. 12

   D. 15

19. (**October 2005**) How many primes are between 30 and 50 (inclusive)?

20. (**October 2005**) Suppose a and b are positive integers such that

$$a^2 - b^2 = 13$$

Then what is ab?

    A. 42

    B. 43

    C. 44

    D. Cannot be determined

21. (**October 2011**) A *perfect square* is a number whose square root is an integer. What is the smallest positive perfect square divisible by 30 and 8?

22. (**Bluebook**) How many numbers from 2 to 35 (inclusive) are a product of two primes?

23. (**Bluebook**) If x, y, z are positive integers such that

$$xyz = 42,$$

then what is the least possible value of $x + y + z$?

    A. 12

    B. 23

    C. 24

    D. 44

24. (**Bluebook**) If a and b are distinct prime numbers, then how many positive factors does

$$a^2 b^2$$

have?

    A. 2

    B. 4

    C. 6

    D. 9

1.4   The Number Line

25. (**March 2005**) Suppose points A, B, C and D lie on a line in that order. If $AC = 12$, $BD = 11$, and $AD = 16$, then what is the length of $\overline{BC}$?

    A. 7

    B. 6

    C. 5

    D. Cannot be determined

26. (**March 2005**) Consider a standard number line with points located at x, x^2, x^3 as shown below.

    Which of the following describe all possible x?

    A. $0 < x < 1$

    B. $-2 < x$

    C. $-1 < x < 0$

    D. No such x exists.

27. (**May 2006**) Suppose the distance between point a and b on a number line is greater than 20. Which of the following must be true?

    I $a < \frac{a+b}{2}$

    II $ab > 400$

    III $20 < |a - b|$

    A. II only

    B. III only

    C. II and III only

    D. I, II, and III.

28. (**October 2006**) Suppose A, B, C, D, and E are points on a line in that order. Moreover, D bisects $\overline{BE}$, C bisects $\overline{AE}$, $BC = 30$, and $AE = 100$. What is the length of $\overline{BD}$?

    A. 10

    B. 40

    C. 50

    D. 60

29. (**May 2007**) Consider the number line below:

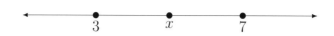

Which of the following must be true?

    I. $x = 5$

   II. $|x - 3| \le |x - 7|$

  III. $|x - 5| < 2$

    A. *I* only

    B. *II* only

    C. *III* only

    D. *II* and *III*.

30. (**October 2008**) Consider the number line marked by points A and B where a and n are positive numbers:

If the distance from A to B is 2^n, then what is the value of a?

    A. $\dfrac{1}{3}$

    B. $\dfrac{1}{2}$

    C. 2

    D. 4

31. (**October 2008**) Suppose an amusement park ride only allow people who are between 60 and 72 inches tall. Which equation represents the height (in inches) of all people who are forbidden to ride?

    A. $|x - 66| > 6$

    B. $|x - 66| < 6$

    C. $|x - 72| < 12$

    D. $|x - 72| > 12$

1.5 Inequalities and Bounds

32. **(March 2005)** If $0 \leq a \leq b$ and
$$a^2 b \leq 125,$$
then what is the biggest possible value of a?

33. **(October 2007)** Given
$$a + ab^2 = 1,$$
what are all possible values of a, given that $b > -1$?

   A. $0 < a \leq .5$

   B. $0 < a \leq 1$

   C. $1 < a \leq 2$

   D. $.5 < a \leq 2$

34. **(May 2008)** For some value of x, suppose that x^2 is the smallest number of the collection
$$\frac{1}{x^3}, \frac{1}{x^2}, \frac{1}{x}, x, x^2$$
and $\frac{1}{x}$ is the largest. Which of the following intervals describe a collection of numbers such that they all satisfy the above condition?

   A. $x > 1$

   B. $0 < x < 1$

   C. $-1 < x < 0$

   D. There is no such x.

35. **(January 2009)** If $x > 100000000$, which of the following is the smallest?

   A. $\dfrac{x}{10^3}$

   B. $\dfrac{x-5}{10^2}$

   C. $\dfrac{\sqrt[3]{x^2}}{\sqrt{x}}$

   D. $\dfrac{\sqrt{x}}{10}$

36. **(January 2010)** For a positive number y, suppose

$$3x + y \geq 6$$

for some x. What is one possible x that satisfies this inequality?

   A. $2 - \dfrac{1}{4}y$

   B. $2 - \dfrac{1}{2}y$

   C. $2 - y$

   D. $2 - 2y$

37. **(October 2011)** If $x > 10000$, what is the expression

$$\frac{x}{xy + 1}$$

closest to?

   A. y

   B. $1 + y$

   C. $\dfrac{1}{y}$

   D. y^2

1.6   Digits and Decimal Expansions

38. **(May 2005)** How many 3 digit combinations are there such that:

- Each digit is an odd number
- If 3 is used, 9 cannot be used.
- The digits, when read left to right, is strictly increasing.

39. **(May 2006)** How many three digit numbers less than 200 are there such that the digits are in strictly increasing order?

   A. 28

   B. 29

   C. 30

   D. 31

40. (**October 2006**) What is the largest four digit number that satisfies the following conditions:

   - The product of the digits is odd.
   - The third digit is one more than the sum of the first two .
   - Each digit is distinct

41. (**May 2008**) Suppose that k is a positive number that has 2 as the hundredth digit in its decimal representation. Then what is the biggest possible value of

$$\frac{k+1}{k}$$

   A. 1
   B. 2
   C. 50
   D. 51

42. (**May 2010**). What is the smallest four digit number such that its digits are distinct, is divisible by 5, and the product of its non-zero digits is divisible by 3 and 4?

43. (**October 2012**) Let A and B represent digits. If

$$99A2$$

leaves a remainder of 7 when divided by 9, then what is the value of A?

   A. 3
   B. 4
   C. 5
   D. 6

44. (**Bluebook**) Consider the number,

$$12345$$

How many ways can you rearrange the digits of this number so that 2 is not the second digit?

   A. 24
   B. 96
   C. 100
   D. 120

1.7   Sequences and Patterns

45. **(May 2006)** A 190 link chain is designed using red and blue links. The pattern alternates between a group of 15 red links followed by a group of y blue links. If the pattern begins and ends with a group of red links and there are 5 group of blue links, then what is the value of y?

    A. 20

    B. 25

    C. 30

    D. 35

46. **(May 2007)** Consider the sequence where each subsequent term is one less than the negative of the preceding term. If the first term of the sequence is 120, then how many of the first 60 terms are less than 100?

47. **(May 2007)**
$$1010010001000\ldots$$

    In the above sequence, we have a 1 followed by 1 zero, a 1 followed by 2 zeros, a 1 followed by 3 zeros, and so on. How many 0's are there among the first 50 terms?

    A. 39

    B. 40

    C. 41

    D. 42

48. **(October 2007)** A chain is designed using red, green, blue, and yellow links. A red link is always followed by a green link, a green link is always followed by a blue link, a blue link is always followed by a yellow link, and a yellow link is always followed by a red link. If the 391th link is blue, what is the color of the first link?

    A. Red

    B. Green

    C. Blue

    D. Yellow

49. **(January 2009)** Consider a sequence in which every term after the second is the product of the two preceding terms. If the first term of the sequence is 1, the second and third terms are negative, and the fourth term is 9, then what is the ninth term of this sequence?

    A. -3

    B. -3^{13}

    C. -3^{21}

    D. 3^{21}

1.8 Counting

50. **(October 2008)** Suppose a four letter word is created by choosing the first (different) letters from the set

$$A = \{a, b, c, d\}$$

and then choosing 2 different letters from the set

$$B = \{g, h, i\}.$$

For example, one can choose the letters a and b from A and b and g and h from B to make the word *bahg*. How many words can one make?

51. **(January 2009)** In a basketball tournament there are 8 teams. If each team plays 4 matches with every other team in 4 matches, then how many matches are there?

52. **(October 2009)** How many integers from 0 to 1800 (inclusive) are NOT divisible by 4?

   A. 1450

   B. 1451

   C. 1452

   D. 1453

Chapter 2

Algebra

2.1 Exponent Properties

1. (**March 2005**) For real numbers a, b, c and d, suppose

$$\begin{aligned} c^a &= d \\ d^b &= c \end{aligned}$$

Which of the following must be the value of c^{ba}

A. 1

B. -1

C. c

D. None of the above

2. (**October 2005**) Which of the following is equivalent to
$$3^x 2^{100} - 3^x 2^{99}$$

A. 3^x

B. $3^x - 2$

C. $3^x - 2^{99}$

D. $3^x \cdot 2^{99}$

3. (**November 2005**) If
$$x^{-2} y^6 = 125,$$

then what is

$$\frac{\sqrt[3]{x^2}}{y^2}$$

4. (**December 2005**) Suppose
$$a = 2^{100} - 2^{99}$$

Then what is $a - 2^{99}$?

    A. 0

    B. 2

    C. 2^{99}

    D. 2^{100}

5. (**October 2007**) If
$$3^a \cdot 3^b = 729$$
$$\frac{3^a}{3^b} = 9$$

for real numbers a and b, what is the value of a?

    A. 2

    B. 4

    C. 6

    D. 8

6. (**May 2010**). Which of the following is the same as
$$(a^n b^n)^2 + (ab)^{n+3}$$

    A. $(ab)^n((ab)^n + 1)$

    B. $(ab)^{n+3}((ab)^{n-3} + 1)$

    C. $(ab)^{2n}$

    D. $(ab)^{2n}(1 + ab)$

7. (**October 2011**) Let a, b and c be positive numbers. If
$$4^a = 9b$$
$$2^a = 3c$$

then what is b in terms of c?

    A. c

    B. $\sqrt{c}$

    C. c^2

    D. $3c$

8. (**Bluebook**) For some real numbers x, y, a and b, suppose

$$\begin{aligned} x^{1/3} &= \sqrt{a} \\ y^{-1/2} &= \sqrt[4]{b} \end{aligned}$$

Which of the following must be the same as $\dfrac{x}{y}$?

  A. ab

  B. $a\sqrt{ab}$

  C. $a\sqrt{\dfrac{a}{b}}$

  D. None of the above

2.2   Word Problems

9. (**March 2005**) Suppose that, on an exam, the class average of n students is 90. However, 6 students were caught cheating and their scores were replaced with 0's. If the class average dropped to 50, which of the following gives the average of the 6 students who cheated prior to getting caught?

  A. $6n$

  B. $\dfrac{19n}{3}$

  C. $\dfrac{20n}{3}$

  D. $7n$

10. (**March 2005**) For positive real numbers a, b, c and d, we know that a percent of b percent is the same as c percent of d. What is d in terms of a, b and c?

  A. $\frac{ab}{c}$

  B. $\frac{ab}{100c}$

  C. $\frac{ab}{1000c}$

  D. $\frac{ab}{10000c}$

11. (**March 2005**) The cost for a taxi is a dollars for the first b miles and c dollars for every d miles beyond the first b miles. What is the cost of a 28-mile trip in terms of a, b, c and d?

  A. $a + \frac{28c}{d}$

  B. $a + \frac{c(28-b)}{d}$

  C. $c + \frac{28b}{a}$

  D. $c + \frac{b(28-d)}{a}$

12. **(May 2005)** Alice and Bob are standing at diametrically opposite ends of a circular racetrack:

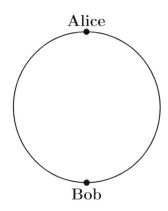

From this starting position, they each walk with steps of constant length. If Alice takes 21 steps clockwise and Bob takes 4 steps clockwise, then they will meet up at the same position. However, if, from the starting position, Alice takes 6 steps clockwise and Bob takes 6 steps counterclockwise, then they will also meet up at the same position. How many steps will it take Bob to walk the entire track by himself?

   A. 20

   B. 50

   C. 77

   D. 100

13. **(November 2005)** Suppose there are 10 red socks, 11 white socks, and 12 blue socks in a drawer. If Dobby draws socks from the drawer at random, then what is the least number of socks he needs to draw to guarantee he has one of each color?

   A. 3

   B. 22

   C. 24

   D. 33

14. (**December 2005**) Consider a chessboard that alternates in color. For example, the image below is a standard chessboard with 8 rows and 8 columns in which the upper left corner is white:

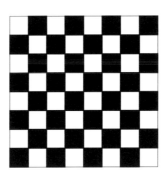

In a chessboard with 21 rows, 21 columns, and upper left corner colored white, how many black tiles are on the outer edge of this chessboard?

15. (**December 2005**) In a jar, there are 30 red jelly beans, 20 white jelly beans, and 10 green jelly beans. If we are to add x green jelly beans, then how many do we need to add so the probability of randomly drawing a green jelly bean is $\frac{1}{2}$?

16. (**October 2006**) Suppose a $10000 car has its price increased by p percent and then decreased by p percent. What is the final price of the car?

   A. 10000

   B. $10000(1 - p^2)$

   C. $10000(1 + p^2)$

   D. $10000 - p^2$

17. (**May 2007**) Suppose 80 dollar bills are divided among Alice, Bob, Capucine, Derrick, Eric, and Fiona. If Alice receives more money than any other person, then what is the least number of dollars that Alice can receive?

18. **(May 2007)** Fiona has a colored egg collection. Suppose three quarters of her eggs are blue. Moreover, a sixth of her blue eggs are not ostrich eggs. If she has ten blue ostrich eggs, then how many eggs does she have?

    A. 12

    B. 14

    C. 15

    D. 16

19. **(May 2007)** In the Garcia family, Miguel is a brother of Lucy. If Miguel has two more brothers than sisters and the number of brothers that Lucy has is triple the number of sisters, then how many siblings does Lucy have?

20. **(October 2007)** Suppose there are 120 fish in a tank. If half the fish are striped and three quarters of the fish are blue, which of the following numbers cannot be the number of fish that are striped and blue?

    A. 20

    B. 30

    C. 50

    D. 60

21. **(January 2008)** Suppose Danny travels from home to work. For the first half of his journey, Danny travels at 20mph. For the next quarter of his journey, he travels at 30mph. For the last quarter of his journey, he travels at 40mph. If the total time of Danny's journey was 2 hours, what is his average speed (in miles per hour)?

    A. 27.5

    B. 30

    C. 30.5

    D. 50

22. **(January 2008)** A dumbbell rack holds a collection of weights. There are 5 two pound weights, 4 three pound weights, 6 five pound weights, x 10 pound weights, and 5 twenty pound weights. If the median weight on the rack is 10 pounds, what is the smallest number that x can be?

    A. 10

    B. 11

    C. 12

    D. 14

23. (**October 2008**) Suppose we have a collection of n distinct numbers such that the average of the numbers in this set is 42. Suppose we add 12 to the largest element in this collection and subtract 12 from the smallest. Then we replace each number x in the collection with $2x + 5$. What is the new average of the numbers in this collection?

24. (**October 2009**) There are two containers each containing a mixture composed of alcohol and water. We also know that the volume of the mixture in the second container is double that of the volume of the first. If the first container's mixture is composed of three fourths alcohol and the second container mixture is composed of one third water, then what is the ratio of alcohol to water when both mixtures are combined?

    A. $\frac{11}{25}$

    B. $\frac{25}{11}$

    C. $\frac{2}{5}$

    D. $\frac{5}{2}$

25. (**October 2011**) What is the greatest number of Thursdays that could occur in a 365 day year?

    A. 51

    B. 52

    C. 53

    D. 54

26. (**October 2012**) To ride a taxi using company A is \$10 for the first 5 miles and \$3 per mile for each mile after the first five. Taxi company B; however, charges \$55 for the first 10 miles and \$1 per mile after the first 10. If both taxi companies charge the same amount for a particular ride, what must be the length (in miles) of that taxi ride?

    A. 15

    B. 20

    C. 25

    D. 30

27. (**Bluebook**) Starting at opposite ends of a straight highway, Fiona drives towards Elaine at 20mph and Elaine drives towards Fiona at 30mph. If the length of the highway is 75 miles, then how many minutes do they each have to drive before they meet up?

    A. 80

    B. 90

    C. 100

    D. 110

28. **(Bluebook)** At a testing center, students can take a test in either Room A or Room B. If each room must have at least two people each, then how many ways can 5 students be distributed among these two rooms?

    A. 19

    B. 20

    C. 21

    D. 22

2.3   Factoring

29. **(December 2005)** If

$$\begin{aligned} x^2 + y^2 &= 52 \\ xy &= 24 \end{aligned}$$

Then what is $(x - y)^2$?

30. **(October 2008)** If

$$\frac{a - b}{a^2 - b^2} = \frac{1}{5}$$

and

$$\frac{a^2 - b^2}{a + b} = 1,$$

then what is b?

31. **(May 2010).** If

$$x^2 = y^2$$

what must be true?

    I. $x = y$

   II. $xy > 0$

  III. If $x - y > 0$, then $x + y = 0$.

    A. *I* only

    B. *III* only

    C. *I* and *II* only.

    D. *I*, *II*, and *III*.

32. **(Bluebook)** If
$$a^2b - ab^2 = 30$$
$$ab = 6$$

then what is $b - a$?

   A. -5

   B. 5

   C. 10

   D. Cannot be determined

2.4   Functions

33. **(January 2006)** For any non-negative numbers x and y such that x and y are not both zero, define the operation
$$x \Delta y = x^y + y^x$$

Which of the following are always true for positive numbers a and b?

   I. $a \Delta b = b \Delta a$

   II. $0 \Delta b = 1$

   III $a \Delta 1 - b \Delta 1 = a - b$

   A. *I* only

   B. *I* and *II* only

   C. *I* and *III* only

   D. *I, II* and *III*

34. **(October 2006)** Let
$$f(x) = a(x-5)(x-2)(x-1)$$

for some $a > 0$. If $f(2t+5) = 0$, then what is the biggest possible value of t?

35. **(October 2006)** Consider the quadratic
$$f(x) = x^2 - 16x + k$$

where k is some constant. If
$$f(3) = f(s)$$

for some $s \neq 3$, then what is the value of s?

36. (**May 2007**) For every x, suppose

$$x^2 - (x-5)(x-3) = ax + b + bx.$$

What is the value of a?

37. (**May 2007**) We say that a function satisfies the *superposition principle* if

$$f(x+y) = f(x) + f(y)$$

for every x and y. Which of the following functions satisfies the *superposition principle*?

A. $f(x) = 3x + 1$

B. $f(x) = x^2$

C. $f(x) = 3x$

D. $f(x) = 1$

38. (**May 2007**) Suppose

$$f(x+y) = f(x) + f(y)$$

for every x and y. What must be true?

I. $f(0) = 0$

II. $f(1) = 1$

III. $f(2x) = 2f(x)$

A. *I* only

B. *I* and *II* only

C. *I* and *III* only

D. *I, II* and *III*

39. (**October 2007**) In the figure below, right triangle $\triangle ABC$ has one side on the x-axis and two vertices that lie on the graph of $f(x) = 2x^2 - 11x + 12$. If the slope of $\overline{AC}$ is 2, what is the area of $\triangle ABC$?

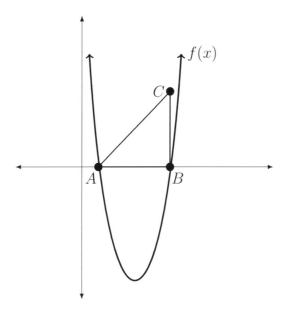

    A. 2.5

    B. 3

    C. 6

    D. 6.25

40. (**January 2008**) Consider the function

$$f(n) = (n - 10)(n - 5)(n - 1)$$

For how many positive integers n is $f(n)$ negative?

    A. 4

    B. 6

    C. 7

    D. 8

41. (**October 2008**) Which of the following functions satisfies the property

$$f(-x) = f(x)$$

for every x?

    A. $f(x) = |x - 2| + x^2$

    B. $f(x) = x + |x^3|$

    C. $f(x) = |x| + 3^x$

    D. $f(x) = |x^3| + |x^5|$

42. **(May 2009)** For some positive integer k, the quadrilateral $ABCD$ has three vertices on the quadratic $f(x) = x^2 - k^2$ as shown below:

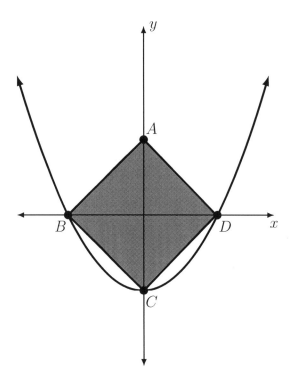

If $\overline{BD}$ bisects $\overline{AC}$, which of the following is a possible area for quadrilateral $ABCD$?

A. .30

B. .36

C. 72

D. 100

43. **(October 2011)** Let
$$f(x) = b^x$$
where b is a positive integer. Which of the following is the same as $f(x + y)$?

A. $f(x) + f(y)$

B. $f(x)f(y)$

C. $f(x)^y$

D. $f(x)y$

44. **(October 2012)** For some positive number k, the quadratic $f(x) = (x - k)(x + k)$ is graphed below:

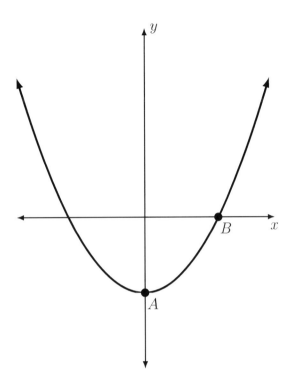

If the slope of $\overline{AB}$ (not shown) is 4, then what is k?

A. .25

B. .5

C. 2

D. 4

45. **(Bluebook)** Suppose $f(x)$ and $g(x)$ are quadratics with vertices marked below:

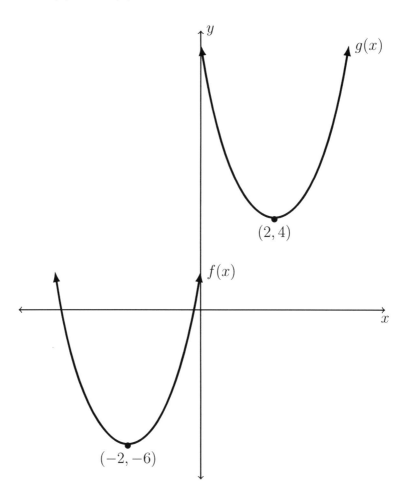

If
$$g(x) = f(x + c) + d$$
then what is the value of cd?

    A. -40

    B. 0

    C. 20

    D. 40

2.5 Directly Proportional and Inversely Proportional

46. **(May 2007)** If x and y are positive and x is directly proportional to y^2, then $\dfrac{1}{y}$ is inversely proportional to which of the following?

    A. $\sqrt{x}$

    B. x^2

    C. $\dfrac{1}{x}$

    D. $\dfrac{1}{\sqrt{x}}$

47. **(May 2009)** Let $x - 1$ be inversely proportional to $2y$. Suppose we know that when x is $a + 1$, then $y = b$. Moreover, when y is a, then x is $b + 2$. What is the value of a?

2.6 System of Equations

48. **(October 2007)** If

$$\begin{aligned} -a + b + c &= 3 \\ a - b + c &= 4 \\ a + b - c &= 5 \end{aligned}$$

then what is $a + b + c$?

    A. 6

    B. 7

    C. 12

    D. 15

49. **(May 2010)** If

$$\begin{aligned} 3x - 2y + z &= 12 \\ x - y + z &= 5 \end{aligned}$$

then what is $x - z$?

    A. 2

    B. 7

    C. 10

    D. Cannot be determined

50. **(Bluebook)** If

$$a + b = 8$$
$$b + c = 12$$
$$c + d = 18$$

then what is $a + d$?

    A. 12

    B. 13

    C. 14

    D. Cannot be determined

Chapter 3

Geometry

3.1 Coordinate Geometry

1. **(May 2006)** Let $f(x) = mx + b$ for some m and b. If $f(3) = 10$, which of the following cannot be true?

    A. $f(1) = 12$ and $f(5) = 8$

    B. $f(2) = 12$ and $f(4) = 10$

    C. $m = 0$

    D. $b = 0$

2. **(May 2006)** If the area of $\triangle ACD$ is 100 and B is the midpoint of $\overline{AC}$, then what is the (x, y) coordinate of B?

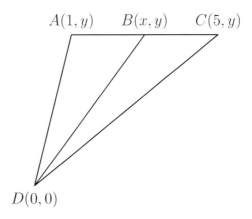

$A(1, y)$ $\quad$ $B(x, y)$ $\quad$ $C(5, y)$

$D(0, 0)$

    A. $(2.5, 50)$

    B. $(2.5, 25)$

    C. $(3, 50)$

    D. $(3, 25)$

3. **(October 2012)** Consider the following segment $\overline{AB}$:

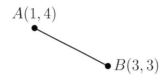

If $\overline{AB}$ is part of square $ABCD$, then what is the slope of $\overline{BC}$?

    A. .5

    B. 2

    C. 2.5

    D. Cannot be determined.

4. **(October 2012)** Suppose the coordinate $(3, 0)$ is shifted four units to the right and two units up, and then rotated $90°$ counterclockwise about the point $(5, 2)$. If the new point is (x, y), then what is $x + y$?

    A. 5

    B. 7

    C. 9

    D. 11

3.2 Planar Geometry

5. **(January 2006)** Suppose we have a polygon with all equal angles and all equal sides centered at the point C. From vertices A and D of this polygon, we can cut out the quadrilateral $ABDC$:

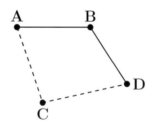

If $m\angle ACD = 90°$, how many sides did the uncut polygon originally have?

    A. 5

    B. 6

    C. 7

    D. 8

6. **(October 2008)** Suppose $ABCD$ and $CFGH$ are rectangles.

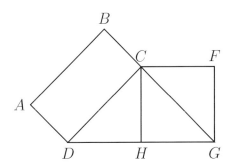

Which of the following must be true?

    A. $m\angle CDH = m\angle FCG$

    B. $m\angle CDH = m\angle CGH$

    C. $m\angle DCH = m\angle HCG$

    D. $m\angle CDH = m\angle CGF$

7. **(October 2008)** Let a, b, c, d, e, and f be distinct lines. If

$$
\begin{aligned}
a &\parallel b, \\
b &\perp c, \\
c &\parallel d, \\
d &\perp e, \\
e &\parallel f
\end{aligned}
$$

then how many of the aforementioned lines are perpendicular to a?

8. **(October 2009)** How many line segments are there that connect two midpoints of two sides of an octagon?

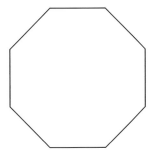

9. **(October 2009)** Suppose you have three concentric squares with center at B. Moreover, the middle square has double the area of the innermost square, and the outermost square has double the area of the middle square. If the sum of the lengths of $\overline{AB}$ and $\overline{BC}$ (not drawn) is $12\sqrt{2}$, then what is the area of the innermost square?

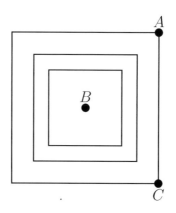

   A. 3.25

   B. 6

   C. 9

   D. 36

10. **(May 2010)** On the Cartesian plane below, consider line segment $\overline{AB}$:

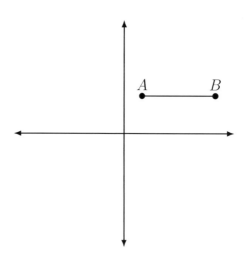

How many points C are on the plane such that $AC = CB$.

   A. 1

   B. 2

   C. 4

   D. More than 4

3.3 Triangles

11. (**March 2005**) The right triangles $\triangle ABC$ and $\triangle MBN$ are shown below. If M is the midpoint of side $\overline{AB}$, N is the midpoint of $\overline{AC}$, and $m\angle ACB = 30°$, then what fraction of triangle $\triangle ABC$ is shaded?

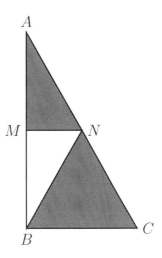

12. (**March 2005**) Suppose $m\angle ACB = 90°$ and $m\angle ACD = m\angle BCD$. If $AB = 10$ and $AC = CB$, then which of the following can be a value for BD?

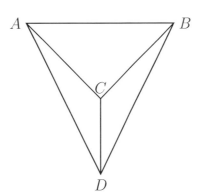

    A. 4

    B. 5

    C. 7

    D. 9

13. **(May 2005)** A 13 feet ladder is leaning against a wall that is perpendicular to the ground. After the ladder slips, the top of the ladder falls 7 feet along the wall. If the base of the ladder is currently 12 feet from the wall, how far (in feet) did the base of the ladder move away from the wall after it slipped?

14. **(December 2005)** Let $\overline{BC}$ be parallel to $\overline{DE}$. Moreover, $BC = 5$ and $DE = 10$. Then what is the ratio of AB to BD?

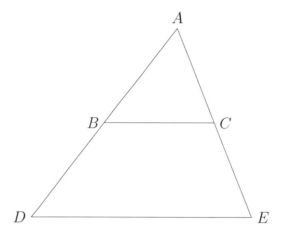

15. **(May 2006)** If $\triangle ABC$ has sides of integer length, and $AB = BC = 12$, then how many different possible lengths can $\overline{CD}$ have?

    A. 22

    B. 23

    C. 24

    D. 25

16. **(May 2006)** In $\triangle ABC$,

$$
\begin{aligned}
AB &= 5 \\
BC &= 6 \\
AC &= 5
\end{aligned}
$$

What must be true about the measure of $\angle BAC$?

    A. $180° > m\angle BAC > 90°$

    B. $90° > m\angle BAC > 60°$

    C. $60° > m\angle BAC > 40°$

    D. $m\angle BAC = m\angle ABC$

17. (**October 2006**) $\triangle ABC$ and $\triangle GHI$ are equilateral triangles with perimeter 9 and triangle $\triangle DEF$ is an equilateral triangle with perimeter 12. If $AI = 8$ and $DC = GF$, then what is the perimeter of the bolded region?

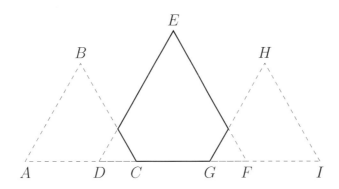

18. (**October 2006**) Let $ABCD$ be a rectangle with $AB = 6\sqrt{3}$ and $AD = 4$. Moreover, $m\angle BEC = 30°$. What is the total area of the shaded regions?

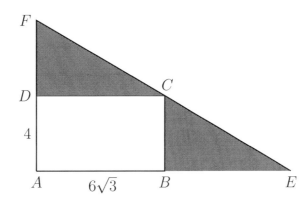

A. $23\sqrt{3}$

B. $24\sqrt{3}$

C. $25\sqrt{3}$

D. $26\sqrt{3}$

19. (**January 2008**) Consider the isoceles triangle $\triangle ABC$. If one pair of angles has a measure whose sum is 160°, then what is the largest possible angle that $\triangle ABC$ can have?

A. 60°

B. 80°

C. 100°

D. 140°

20. **(October 2008)** Suppose $AB = 20$ and the three triangles that lie on $\overline{AB}$ are all equilateral. What is the sum of the perimeters of these three triangles?

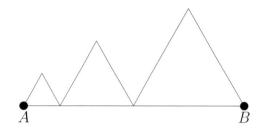

21. **(October 2009)** In the figure below, $\overline{BC}$ is parallel to $\overline{DE}$. If $AC = 6$, $DE = 18$, and $CE = 12$, then what is the length of $\overline{BC}$?

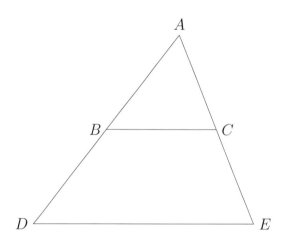

    A. 6

    B. 9

    C. 10

    D. 36

22. (**January 2010**) The length of $\overline{AC}$ in the cube below is 2.

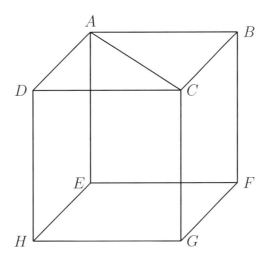

What is the perimeter of the triangle formed by connecting vertices A, C and H?

   A. 6

   B. 8

   C. 10

   D. 12

23. (**October 2012**) Suppose the quadrilateral $ABCD$ has sides that are integers and $AD = 5$ and $BC = 3$. If the diagonal $\overline{AC}$ has a length of 4, what is the greatest possible perimeter that $ABCD$ can have?

   A. 19

   B. 21

   C. 22

   D. 30

24. (**Bluebook**) Consider line segments $\overline{AB}$ and $\overline{BC}$:

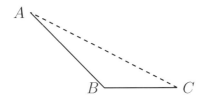

If $\angle ABC$ is chosen such that $\triangle ABC$ has the greatest possible area, which of the following describes $\angle ABC$?

   A. $m\angle ABC = 60°$

   B. $m\angle ABC = 90°$

   C. $m\angle ABC > 90°$

   D. Cannot be determined

3.4   Circles

25. (**May 2005**) If the radius of the circle centered at O is r, $\overline{AOB}$ is a diameter, $AC = 2r - 4$, $BC = 2r - 2$ then what is r?

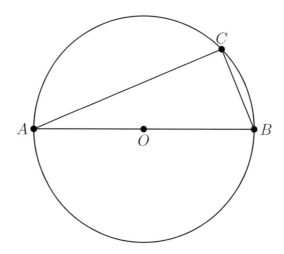

   A. 5

   B. 6

   C. 10

   D. Cannot be determined.

26. (**October 2005**) The area of the semicircle below is 36π. If $BC = AB$, then what is the area of triangle $\triangle ABC$?

   A. 18

   B. 36

   C. 50

   D. Cannot be determined

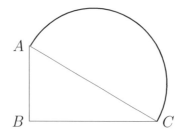

27. (**May 2006**) Lines l and s are tangent to the circle (centered at C) at points A and B.

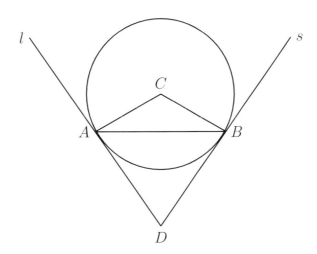

Which of the following must be true?

   I. $m\angle CAB = m\angle ABD$

  II. $m\angle BAD = m\angle ABD$

 III. If $m\angle ACB = 90°$, then quadrilateral $ABCD$ is a rectangle.

  A. I only

  B. II only

  C. III only

  D. II and III only

28. **(January 2007)** The following is an equilateral triangle of perimeter 12 inscribed inside a circle:

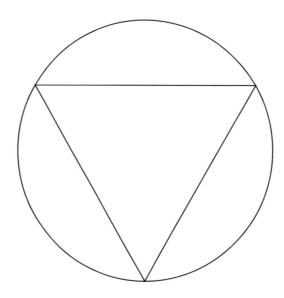

How many equilateral triangles of perimeter 12 can you inscribe within this circle?

A. 2

B. 3

C. 4

D. More than 4

29. **(October 2007)** If $\overline{AB}$ (not drawn) is a diameter of a semicircle, then what is the area of the region below in terms of x?

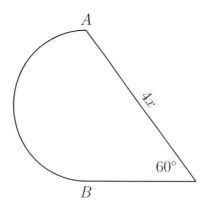

A. $1.5x^2\pi + 2x^2\sqrt{3}$

B. $3x^2\pi + 2x^2\sqrt{3}$

C. $1.5x^2\pi + 4x^2\sqrt{3}$

D. $3x^2\pi + 4x^2\sqrt{3}$

30. **(January 2008)** The figure below has 5 congruent circles that are tangent to each other. Moreover, the figure contains two squares, each with two vertices on the center of circles. If the total area of the five circles is 10π, then what is the difference between the area of the larger square and the area of the smaller square?

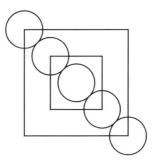

A. 47

B. 48

C. 49

D. 50

31. **(October 2008)** The three circles below are congruent and have radius 3:

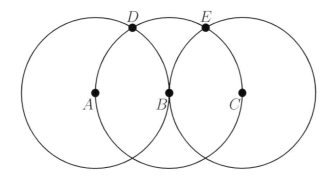

If A, B and C are the centers of the three circles, then what is the perimeter of $\triangle DFE$ (not drawn)?

32. **(October 2008)** In the circle below, the center is at A and the radius is 6. If the measures of arcs $\overset{\frown}{BC}$ and $\overset{\frown}{CD}$ are equal and $m\angle BAD = 120°$, then what is the perimeter of the shaded region?

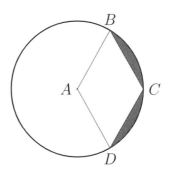

    A. $10 + 2\pi$

    B. $10 + 4\pi$

    C. $12 + 2\pi$

    D. $12 + 4\pi$

33. **(January 2009)** For a circle centered at O, line $\mathcal{L}$ is tangent to this circle at A and has a slope of $-\dfrac{1}{2}$. If the length of $\overline{OB}$ is 2 and $\overline{OB} \perp \overline{AB}$, then what is the radius of the circle?

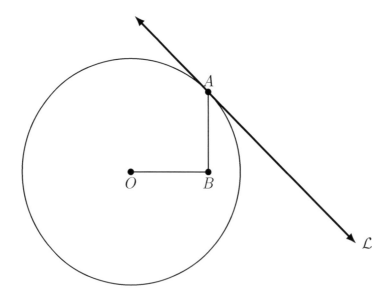

    A. 2

    B. $3\sqrt{2}$

    C. $2\sqrt{5}$

    D. 4

34. **(October 2011)** Suppose a circle has a 60° arc removed. Then, the endpoints of the remaining arc are connected with a line segment to create the following shape:

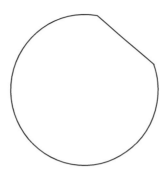

If the original circle had a radius of 6, then what is the perimeter of this shape?

A. 10π

B. $10\pi + 6$

C. 12π

D. $12\pi + 6$

35. **(October 2012)** Suppose we have four colinear points A, B, C and D such that $AB = BC = CD$:

If a circle is to be drawn using one of these points as a center and another as a point on its circumference, then how many circles can be drawn?

A. 8

B. 10

C. 11

D. 12

36. **(October 2012)** Line l is tangent to the circle at point A. If point C is the center of the circle and $m\angle ADC = 30°$, then what is the measure of $\angle ABD$?

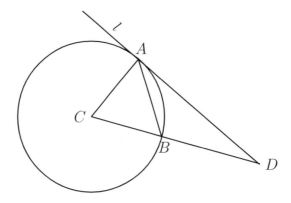

    A. 30°

    B. 60°

    C. 90°

    D. 120°

37. **(Bluebook)** Rectangles $ABCD$ and $EBGH$ are inscribed in the quarter circle centered at B with radius 5.

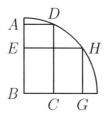

What is the sum of the lengths of the segments (not drawn) $\overline{AC}$ and $\overline{EG}$

    A. 5

    B. 10

    C. 15

    D. 20

38. (**Bluebook**) Square $ABCD$ is composed of 16 identical squares. Moreover, a point is placed in the center of each corner square:

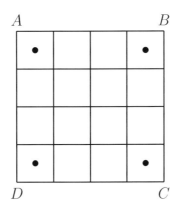

If the area of $ABCD$ is 64, then what is the area of the circle (not shown) that goes through the four points?

   A. 16π

   B. 18π

   C. 20π

   D. 22π

3.5 3D Geometry

39. (**March 2005**) The figure below is a tetrahedron: a pyramid where each side is an equilateral triangle. By connecting edges together, how many 60° angles does a tetrahedron have?

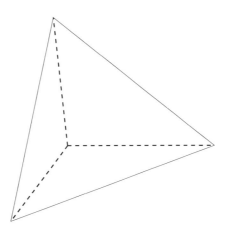

   A. 8

   B. 9

   C. 12

   D. 16

40. (**October 2006**) A cylinder has its height increased by 50% and its radius decreased by 50%. Which of the following must be true?

    A. The cylinder's volume is unchanged.

    B. The cylinder's surface area is unchanged.

    C. The volume is increased by more than 25%

    D. The volume is decreased by more than 25%

41. (**October 2006**) In a right circular cone, suppose that r is the radius of the base. If the diameter of the base and height of the cone have the same length, what is the distance (in terms of r) from C to any point on the circumference of the base?

    A. $r\sqrt{2}$

    B. $r\sqrt{3}$

    C. $r\sqrt{5}$

    D. $2r$

42. (**May 2007**) Consider a sphere inscribed inside a cube. If the sphere has radius r, then what is the length of the longest line segment that can be formed by connecting two of the cube's vertices?

    A. r

    B. $r\sqrt{3}$

    C. $2r$

    D. $2r\sqrt{3}$

43. **(October 2007)** A spherical container of radius r that is completely filled with water is poured into a cylinder of height h and radius r. If, after pouring the water, the cylinder is three quarters full, then what is h in terms of r?(Note: the volume of a sphere is $\frac{4}{3}\pi r^3$.)

    A. r

    B. $\frac{4}{3}r$

    C. $\frac{5}{3}r$

    D. $\frac{16}{9}r$

44. **(January 2008)** A sphere of radius 4 is cut into four equal parts, as shown below:

    How much more surface area does the sum of the surface areas of the four new pieces have when compared to the surface area of the original sphere?

    A. 0

    B. 16π

    C. 32π

    D. 64π

45. **(October 2009)** The radius of a cylinder is double its height. In terms of radius r, what is the surface area of the cylinder?

    A. $\frac{\pi r^3}{2}$

    B. $3\pi r^2$

    C. $4\pi r^2$

    D. $6\pi r^2$

46. **(May 2010)**. A cylinder has a radius of 100 decimeters and a height of 5π decimeters. What is this cylinder's volume in meters? (1 meter = 10 decimeters).

47. **(October 2012)** A cube of surface area 54 in^2 is composed of 27 smaller identical cubes. If the eight corner cubes are removed, what is the new surface area (in square inches)?

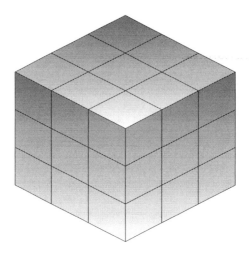

   A. 50

   B. 54

   C. 58

   D. 62

48. **(Bluebook)** Consider the wooden $4 \times 4 \times 4$ cube composed of smaller $1 \times 1 \times 1$ cubes:

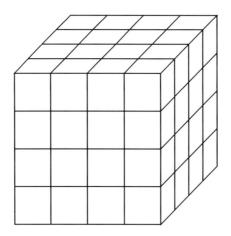

   If the outer layer of the $4 \times 4 \times 4$ cube is painted black, then, when disassembled, how many of the $1 \times 1 \times 1$ cubes are painted black?

Chapter 4

Answer Key

Numbers

Integers

1. C

2. D

3. D

4. 1

5. B

6. 5

7. A

8. 3

9. A

10. C

11. D

12. D

Evens and Odds

13. A

14. 50

15. A

16. C

17. C

Primes

18. B

19. 5

20. A

21. 3600

22. 13

23. A

24. D

The Number Line

25. A

26. D

27. B

28. B

29. C

30. A

31. A

Inequalities and Bounds

32. 5

33. B

34. D

35. C

36. A

37. C

Digits and Decimal Expansions

38. 7

39. A

40. 7195

41. D

42. 1260

43. C

44. B

Sequences and Patterns

45. A

46. 30

47. B

48. D

49. C

Counting

50. 72

51. 112

52. B

Algebra

Exponent Properties

1. C
2. D
3. .2
4. A
5. B
6. B
7. C
8. B

Word Problems

9. C
10. B
11. B
12. A
13. C
14. 40
15. 40
16. D
17. 15
18. D
19. 8
20. A
21. A
22. B
23. 89
24. B

25. C
26. C
27. B
28. B

Factoring

29. 4
30. 2
31. B
32. A

Functions

33. D
34. 0
35. 13
36. 23
37. C
38. C
39. D
40. A
41. D
42. C
43. B
44. D
45. A

Directly Proportional and Inversely Proportional

46. A
47. 0

System of Equations

48. C
49. A
50. C

Geometry

Coordinate Geometry

1. B

2. C

3. B

4. C

Planar Geometry

5. D

6. D

7. 2

8. 28

9. C

10. D

Triangles

11. $\frac{3}{4}$

12. D

13. 7

14. 1

15. B

16. B

17. 10

18. D

19. D

20. 60

21. A

22. A

23. C

24. B

Circles

25. A

26. A

27. D

28. D

29. A

30. B

31. 9

32. D

33. C

34. B

35. B

36. D

37. B

38. B

3D Geometry

39. C

40. D

41. C

42. D

43. D

44. C

45. B

46. 50

47. B

48. 56

Made in the USA
Monee, IL
05 November 2019